Class Clown Chronicles:
Hilarious Jokes for Kids

Sabat Beatto

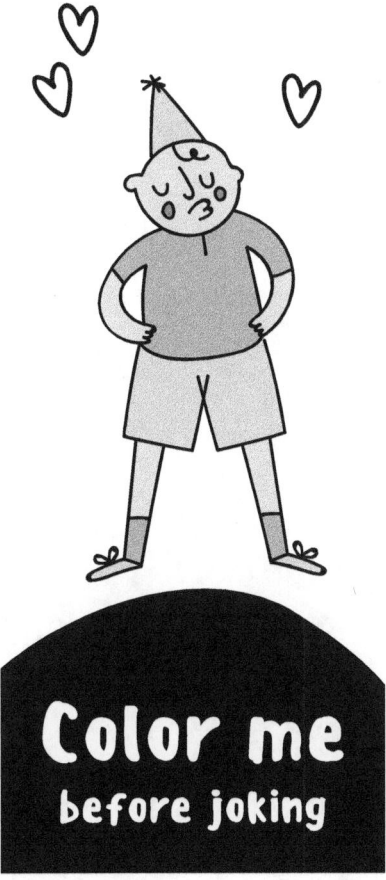

Color me
before joking

Class Clown Chronicles:
Hilarious Jokes for Kids

To
Steven Lopez

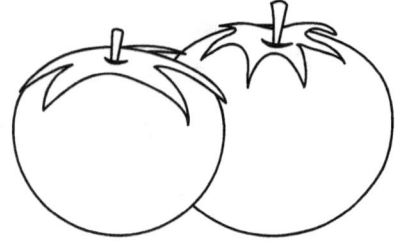

Why did the
tomato turn red?
Because it saw the
salad dressing!

Knock, knock!
Who's there?
Boo.
Boo who?
Don't cry, it's
just a joke!

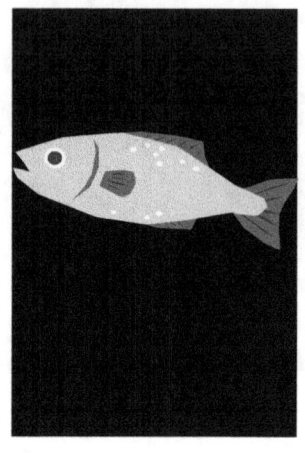

What do you
call a fish that
wears a bowtie?
Sofishticated!

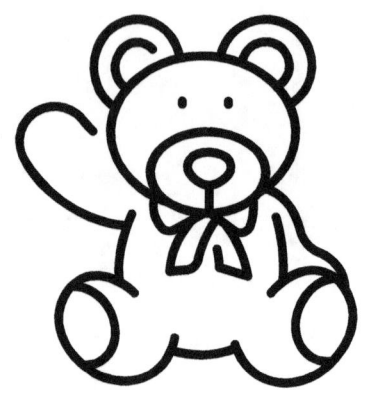

Why did the teddy
bear say no to
dessert?
Because it was
already stuffed!

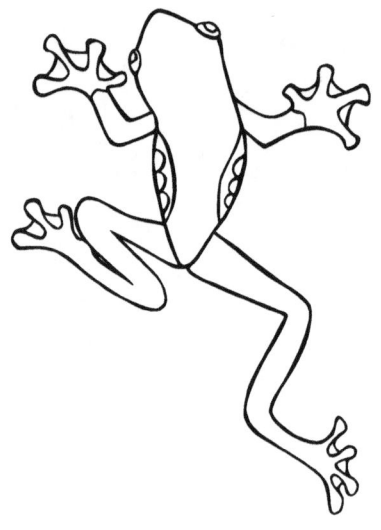

What kind of
shoes do frogs
wear?
Open-toad!

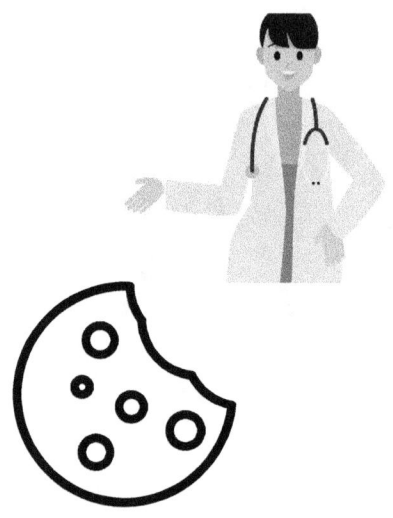

Why did the
cookie go to the
doctor?
Because it felt
crummy!

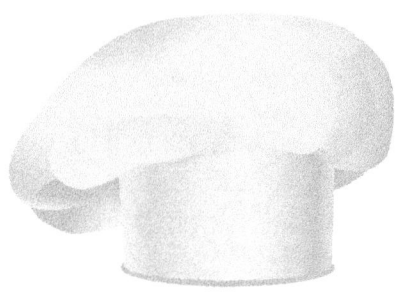

What did one hat
say to the other?
You stay here, I'll
go on ahead!

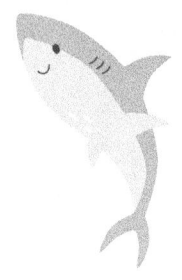

What do you get
when you cross a
snowman and a
shark?
Frostbite!

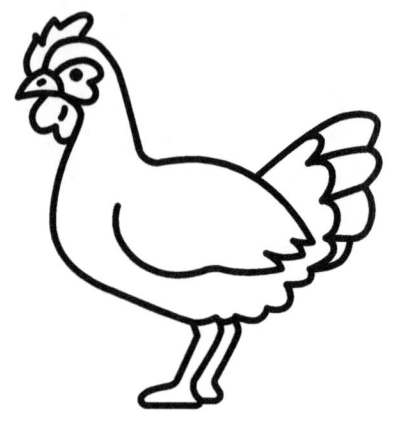

Why did the
chicken cross the
playground?
To get to the other
slide!

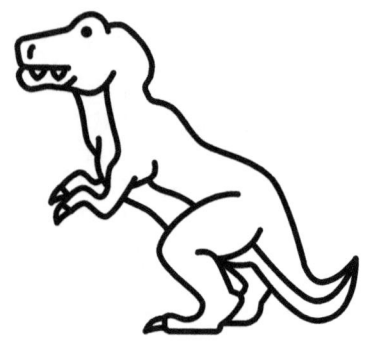

What do you call a
dinosaur that is
sleeping?
A dino-snore!

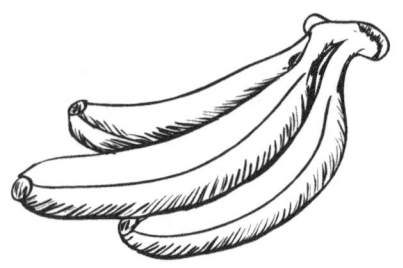

Why did the
banana go to the
doctor?
Because it wasn't
peeling well!

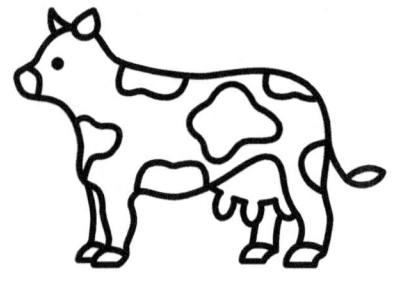

What do you call a
cow that plays an
instrument?
A moosician!

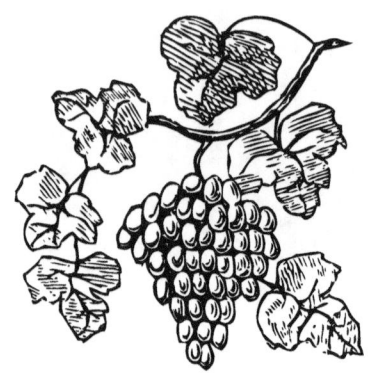

What did the
grape say when it
got stepped on?
Nothing, it just let
out a little wine!

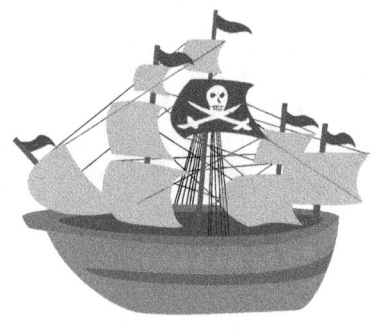

Why did the pirate
take a shower?
To wash his booty!

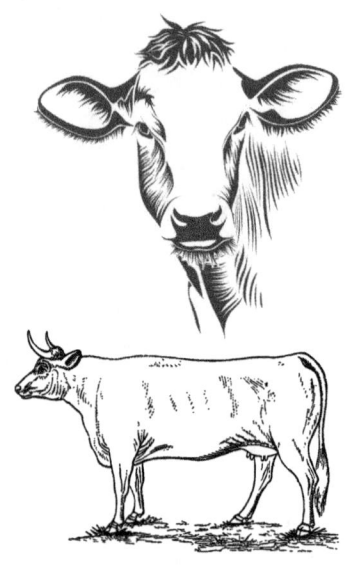

What do you call a
group of cows
playing
instruments?
A moo-sical band!

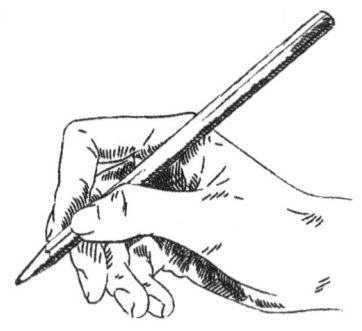

Why did the pencil
cross the road?
To get to the other
point!

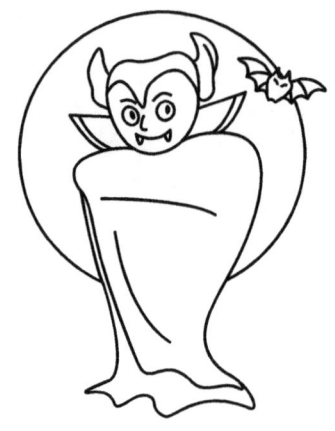

What do you get when you cross a snowman and a vampire? Frostbite!

What do you get when you cross a snowman and a vampire? Frostbite!

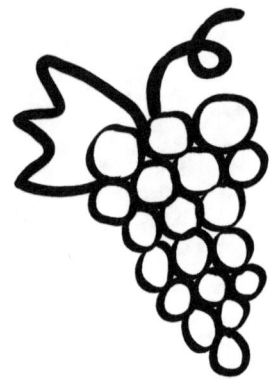

Why did the grape
stop in the middle
of the road?
Because it ran out
of juice!

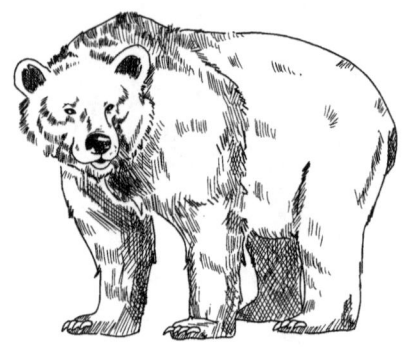

What do you call a
bear with no
teeth?
A gummy bear!

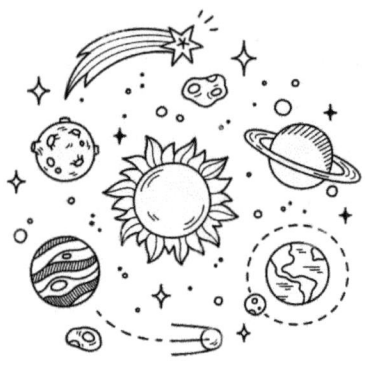

What kind of
music do planets
listen to?
Nep-tunes!

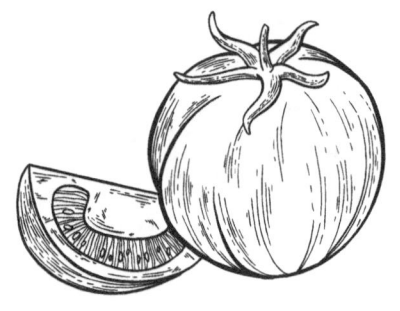

Why did the
tomato turn
green?
Because it saw the
salad dressing
coming!

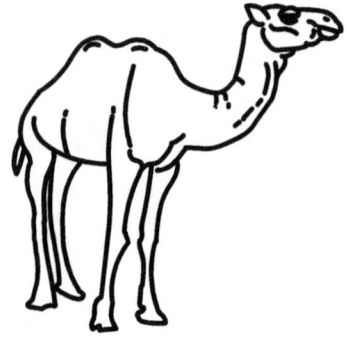

What do you call a camel with three humps? Pregnant!

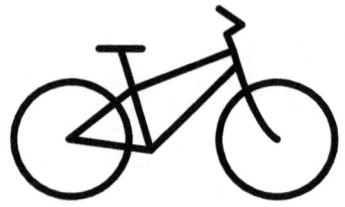

Why did the bike
fall over?
Because it was
two-tired!

Why did the math
book look sad?
Because it had too
many problems!

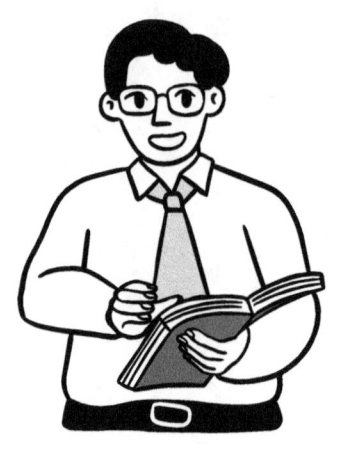

Why did the
teacher wear
sunglasses?
Because her class
was so bright!

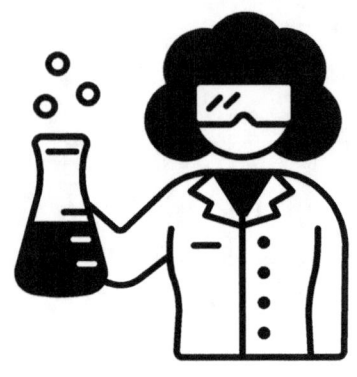

Why don't
scientists trust
atoms?
Because they
make up
everything!

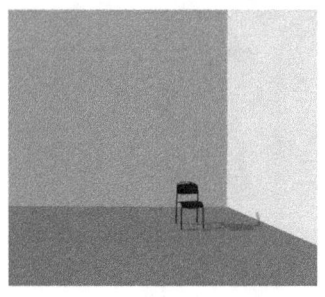

What did one wall
say to the other
wall?
I'll meet you at the
corner!

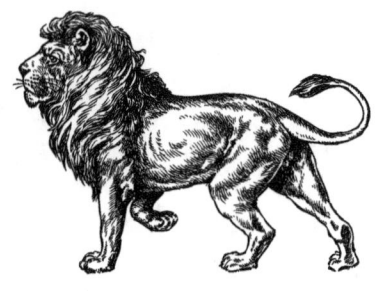

Why did the lion
go to the doctor?
Because he was
feeling a little
roar!

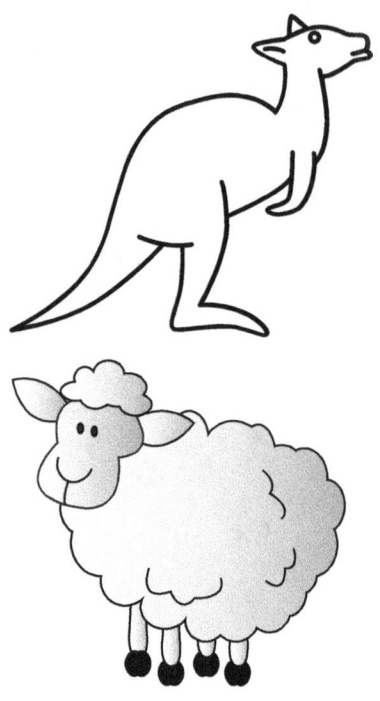

What do you get
when you cross a
sheep and a
kangaroo?
A woolly jumper!